Queen Esther Visits the KING

The Book of Esther for children

Written by Karen Clopton-Dunson

Illustrated by
Michelle Dorenkamp

CONCORDIA PUBLISHING HOUSE · SAINT LOUIS

The people in Susa were weeping.
Queen Esther wanted to know why.
So she sent a messenger
To speak to her cousin Mordecai.

Mordecai said, "We are worried,
And no one knows what to do.
The king has issued a decree
To wipe out every Jew."

Her cousin sent to her these words:
"This news you can't dismiss.
Perhaps God has chosen you
For such a time as this."

"Our people, the Jews, are scared.
They don't want their lives to end.
Esther, you are our queen.
It's you on whom we depend!"

The messenger returned to her.
Esther said, "Tell them not to weep.
I will go visit the king;
That's a promise I will keep."

Then she remembered a rule
That the king wrote for one and all:
"If you want to see the king,
You must wait for his call."

But she refused to wait.
The king she had to see.
So she called in her maids
And gave an urgent plea.

"I need each of you to pray
And turn down every meal.
After three full days,
To the king I will appeal."

Queen Esther soaked in her bath
And slipped on her royal gown.
She sprayed on sweet perfume
And twisted on her crown.

Then Esther went to see the king
Without his invitation.
Her faith in God made her brave
To ask him to save her nation.

The guard checked his list;
Esther's name was not on it.
But she stood there waiting
Till the king allowed her visit.

The king broke a smile
And greeted her with a nod.
The queen let out a sigh
And whispered, "Thank You, God."

The king asked Esther,
"Why are you feeling despair?"
"Please don't destroy the Jews,"
She cried. "Their lives you must spare."

"The Jews will not be slaughtered,"
Was the king's new order.
The queen thanked him softly
And went back to her quarters.

The Jews in the land of Susa
No longer had to weep.
The king made a vow to Esther.
And that promise he did keep.

Like Esther, who had faith in God,
And overcame her fear,
When you pray in Jesus' name,
God will always hear.

Dear Parent,

The king in this Bible story is Ahasuerus, also called Xerxes. He was ruler over Persia, the largest empire in the world at the time. History records that Xerxes was unstable and impetuous.

Esther, chosen for her looks, was just one of his queens. She did not have what we consider today to be a typical wifely relationship with Xerxes. She would not have had the freedom to talk with him whenever she wanted nor to ask him for favors. But the Book of Esther records that she rose to the occasion with diplomacy and success.

The conspiracy against Mordecai and the Jews is an example of how emotions of hatred and jealousy can lead to sin and tragedy and how Satan uses our own human nature against us. God's name is not mentioned in the Book of Esther, but it is clear that He is silently at work. Through Esther, God preserves His people. God is indeed in control of the world's affairs.

While this Arch Book simplifies this event, what we can take away from the biblical account of Esther is that God was at work for the good of His people and that God acted to preserve His people so that the Messiah could be born. Therefore, when you read this story with your child, point out that God works through all situations and all people to accomplish His will.

The Editor